HOW TO BECOME

A SUCCESSFUL MASSAGE THERAPIST

PHAEDRA GEORGIOU DYKE
Dip. LSSM, MISRM

ISBN: 978-1-910662-15-1

First published in 2015

INTRODUCTION

Phaedra qualified as a Swedish Remedial massage therapist in 1985 (as part of the City & Guilds Beauty Therapy Certificate) and worked in North and Central London in salons and clinics as a beauty therapist.

In 1989 she became self-employed and ran a beauty salon within a health club based in Kensington, employing two other staff.

Phaedra left the beauty industry in 1992 to pursue a more sports-related career and joined Central YMCA in London's West End, qualifying as a circuit and weights instructor, teaching classes and individuals. Throughout this time she also managed a fitness team within the facilities department, becoming a pool lifeguard and provided lifeguard training and first aid to staff members.

She continued her management career at Portobello Green Fitness Club (now known as Westway Sports and Fitness) in West London, responsible for gym and studio departments, reception and facilities. In 2003 Phaedra realised that she missed the one-to-one client contact and decided to combine her interests of massage and fitness by studying Sports and Remedial Massage at The London School of Sports Massage in Regents Park, London.

She qualified in 2004 and has worked at various prestigious clinics around London until eventually setting up her own business within Westway Sports and Fitness as a self-employed massage therapist, building up clientele from her previous client lists and the current local area.

In the current climate of job-changing, many people are looking to the health and fitness industry as a way of opting out of office life, and she would like to show you how to make the best possible choice for you as an individual and how to meet your expectations and maximise your success in this wonderful industry!

Phaedra will show you how to choose the right course, how to give yourself the best possible experience whilst you are training and how to decide what type of clients will best meet your needs and expectations.

She now enjoys running a very busy practice and offers you tips and ideas of how to set up, build up and maintain your business, pointing out any potential pitfalls and how to minimise any steep "learning curves".

Phaedra will share some of her own experiences in order to help you be more aware of the ups and downs of running a massage therapy business and getting the best outcomes with minimal set-backs!

PREFACE

My intention at the start of this project was to help those about to start in the therapy industry and those who have just started. I felt that if I had been able to have one-to-one time with an experienced therapist regarding building and maintaining a thriving business, I would have found the following information helpful when I was setting up my business.

I hope the tips and guidance I have shared will help the new therapist avoid the usual pitfalls that might occur and give ideas and suggestions to make the path to a busy practice run smoother than I found it!

Whilst I have tried to give general and unbiased information to cover any massage therapy, my experience naturally swings towards sport and deep tissue remedial work but hopefully this does not colour the relevance of what I am sharing.

The very best of luck to all those individuals choosing massage therapy as their chosen field – I hope you find it as satisfying and rewarding as I have done and continue to do.

Phaedra

CONTENTS

CHAPTER 1

TYPES OF MASSAGE AND COURSES

SELECTING THE TYPE OF MASSAGE

There are such a plethora of massage styles to choose from and many fads that are introduced to the public every few months, but I will cover the tried and tested types of massage that gives you good grounding to build upon if you wish to expand your services. All the pros and cons listed are from the therapist's perspective and consideration.

Swedish remedial

This is one of the most common types of massage and gives the therapist a good foundation for most other massages.

The massage consists of a rhythmic, constant series of massage movements on bare skin for the entire body.

The objective of the massage is to bring about deep relaxation to the client with increased circulation to the muscles and skin and can be conducive in lowering high blood pressure and decreasing stress levels.

Media used are varied and can be talc, cream, oil or wax.

Pros

- *Good foundation to learn most of the other types of massage*
- *Good employment prospects in many industries such as spas, health clubs, home visits.*

Cons

- *Can be monotonous if doing many treatments back to back*
- *If someone has a significant soft tissue problem, Swedish massage will probably give only a very short-term relief.*

Sports massage therapy

A highly effective manual massage that uses advanced soft tissue techniques set within a framework of assessment and rehabilitation procedures to treat pain, reduce symptoms and help recovery of the client's needs.

The massage consists of a wide spectrum of techniques that range in depth and efficacy (releasing, stretching etc). The most common way of delivering the treatment is on bare skin with a small amount of medium but various techniques can also be applied through towels or clothing.

The objective of the massage is specific to the client's needs and the treatment is tailored around these needs. These can range from releasing tight fascia or muscles and reducing scar tissue to improving muscle functionality.

Pros

- *One of the few types of massage that has medical evidence of efficacy, there is a high degree of customer expectation being met and therefore great work satisfaction.*
- *A necessary qualification if you want to work with elite athletes/professional teams.*

Cons

- *Physical fitness of the therapist is highly desirable and a good level of energy and well-being is needed to deliver this type of treatment.*

Bowen Therapy

Each session typically involves gentle rolling motions along the muscles, tendons, and fascia. The therapy's distinctive features are the minimal nature of the physical intervention and pauses incorporated in the treatment. Proponents claim these pauses allow the body to "reset" itself.

The objective is to release and improve the fascial relationship in the body with minimal pressure to allow the body to recharge and balance itself.

Due to the small, light movements, minimal or no medium is used, and can be applied through light clothing.

Pros

- *Easily tolerated movements by the client and no physical demands on the therapist.*
- *Pauses in treatment allow for two or more treatments to be administered at the same time or breaks up treatment for therapist.*

Cons

- *Clients who want to feel deep tissue manipulation are less likely to choose this therapy as effectiveness and improvements are gradual and subtle.*

Thai massage

A series of movements in a firm, rhythmic pressure, following energy lines in the body, applied through clothing.

The objective of the massage is to improve and unblock energy lines (based on acupressure points) to bring about a great sense of well-being and encourages the recipient to become more engaged and energized, for increased mindfulness.

Pros

- *Many well-being centres, spas and clinics are embracing Thai massage so employment choices are varied.*

Cons

- *A very physical type of treatment that requires a good level of fitness of the therapist.*
- *Usual treatment time varies from 90 mins to 2 hours so costings need to reflect how many can be done in a day.*

Reflexology

It involves a pressure technique using the thumbs and fingers on the reflex areas found in the feet and hands. Reflexology is based on the principle that reflexes in the feet and hands correspond to each organ and structure in the body, based on acupressure and massage of Eastern medicine.

The objective of the massage is to unblock the energy lines of the client in order to bring about wellness to the musculo-skeletal and visceral systems.

Pros
- *Therapist can apply most of the treatment seated so not as physically demanding as some other techniques.*

Cons
- *A much more specific type of massage and the client is more likely to request treatment if they have some confidence in Eastern medicine.*

Aromatherapy

A specialised type of massage as, in addition to anatomy and physiology knowledge, the extensive study of oils' efficacy and administration is vital.

Light, specific movements on bare skin using carefully selected oils for the client's needs. This modality is also based on Eastern medicine, working on energy lines in the body.

The objective of this treatment is to bring about improved health and well-being to the client.

Pros
- *A less physically demanding type of massage*
- *Pleasant aromatherapy oils as massage medium for both therapist and client.*

Cons
- *There are very little scientific results to show that oils can provide any physiological benefits to the client.*

COURSE AND COLLEGE SELECTION

Rather than me giving you specific college or course recommendations, I think it would be more beneficial to point out the considerations to take into account when making this important investment in time and money.

What do you want from your qualification?

Do you want to work abroad?

Make sure your certification is recognised in the country in which you are interested in working.

If you are going to be working for a fee (i.e. any paid work) you will need to be insured for personal indemnity and public liability so check with your college that once you are qualified, you are able to get adequate coverage otherwise you will not be allowed to practise.

Is there a certain level of qualification you must reach before you are allowed to treat the public?

Ensure that on completion of your course you are fully qualified – some courses require various levels of certification which can result in very high and unforeseen costs.

How long is the course?

A very short course does not bode well for a thorough coverage of the chosen subject. Quick, intense courses do not leave a lot of time to absorb the course content and leave very little time for hands-on experience, which is absolutely essential for this field of work.

A friend took a two-week sports massage course tacked on to a personal training course – but due to lack of study time and little or no hands-on experience, she finished the course feeling unprepared and lacking confidence to start working on the public and subsequently never used the qualification.

The longer you have to study in between the course delivery, the better it will be for you in the long term, especially if you are new to anatomy and physiology. Background knowledge in these subjects will be invaluable and save you lots of study hours. Ensure you can commit to the hours required to attend college and home study – be realistic and don't underestimate how time-consuming this may be and invest wisely in your course.

Does the college offer good student support?

Check that there will be tutor support outside of college hours as it may be a few weeks before you meet up with a course tutor to ask questions.

Does the college have good connections with insurers, study material suppliers and massage equipment suppliers?

These can all save you time and money and you may be able to get a discount off their product (if not, I have suggested some options at the end of this book).

Different courses obviously require different levels of certification to apply, but a good knowledge of anatomy and physiology or human biology will definitely help you to absorb the course material more easily.

During your course

In addition to the recommended reading by your tutors, read around your subject as much as possible. Sign up to manual therapy sites to receive the latest research or topic and be aware that other therapies can have subjects of interest and relevance – for example, I often visit physiotherapy websites to get further information that my own field may not cover.

Try and experience the actual treatment or similar from a qualified therapist as regularly as possible - being at the "client-end" of the treatment is a valuable lesson (whether it's a positive or negative experience) and will make you a better therapist.

Explore your area and contact your local sports clubs and fitness groups to get some hands-on experience. Offer free treatments to friends and neighbours (you cannot charge a fee to the public without being insured, and you must be qualified to be insured). Bear in mind, however, that once people have had something for free, they're very reticent to then pay for it!

My course required 100 hours of hands-on practice (each client had to be recorded and logged) so I contacted my local American football team called London Blitz and spoke to one of the coaches (thanks, Coach Pierce!) who invited me to their training sessions. I took my couch and parked on the side-lines and treated player after player with a range of injuries, from shoulder injuries to ripped thigh muscles - it was the best experience I could have ever given myself, and the team were benefiting too! I stayed with them for a year and then introduced other students who wanted to take over.

Attend events at which you can set up a treatment area – for example, Help the Aged or Caring for Carers often have events that you can get involved in – you could offer something simple like a hand or foot massage and apart from the practical experience, you help to improve your client/therapist skills too. Check your local council website for upcoming activities and group contact numbers.

Link up with other students on your course to arrange study sessions or just to bounce ideas off one another. I am still in touch with a few ex-students and tutors from all my training and they are the basis of my support network in my professional career.

Examination time!

Many courses assess their students throughout the teaching terms but usually there are some sort of final practical and theoretical assessments. Try and volunteer as a model for other students' exams to get a good idea of what to expect. Generally, massage course content is not something you can "cram" at the last minute - plan your study and revision over the upcoming months and weeks to allow your brain to absorb the information.

With the practical exam, you are either required to bring in your own model or, as in the case of my college, current students volunteered as models (there was always a waiting list!). The examiner will tell you what areas to treat or what ailment to look for on the client. Questions related to this area/ailment are then posed and then another area is given. The examiner is looking for anatomical and physiological knowledge, specialised massage techniques, speed and pressure of massage application and client care.

Remember to be well-prepared, breathe deeply to relax your body – tense arms are terrible for massage, and also slow down your movements - examinees are usually moving too fast because of nerves!

Theory papers are often multiple choice but some work is assessed as you progress through the course. For example, on my course we had three written assignments plus the log book that were completed during the course, and then two theory papers completed under exam conditions.

Remember, preparation is key!

Graduation and beyond

It is at this point that you realise you only know the tip of the iceberg of your field and that there is an abundance of information out there ready to be accessed.

Try not to go post-graduate course crazy straight away! I know of several therapists who kept attending course after course as soon as they qualified but honestly, until you start working on clients, the courses may not seem so relevant. I recommend that you select a maximum of two CPDs (Continual Professional Development) within your first professional year. As you treat clients, the gaps in your knowledge (and there will be), will become more apparent and then course selection will be more appropriate and pertinent.

FIRST AID COURSES

Good colleges usually recommend that you obtain a first aid qualification. This is necessary when you are dealing with the public and especially when it is highly likely that you will be the only other person nearby if something happens to your client during a treatment.

First Aid for Appointed Persons (non-accredited)

Training time usually a half day

Valid for 3 years

This is a non-accredited course (i.e. not recognised by HSE requirements in the workplace) and it is designed for people who work with other individuals who are accredited. This gives you basic first aid but if you are working on your own with clients who may have asthma, diabetes, allergies or heart conditions, then you must have a First Aid at Work qualification.

Emergency First Aid at Work (accredited)

Training time usually 1 day

Valid for 3 years

This is an accredited course and recognised by the HSE as sufficient first aid if you work in a low-risk environment, such as shops, offices and libraries. This course is usually enough for a massage therapist who works from home, mobile work or works within a clinic situation.

First Aid at Work (accredited)

Training time 3 days

Valid for 3 years

This course is designed for those working in a high-risk environment such as construction, manufacturing or chemical plants.

There are also courses specifically for Sports First Aid and is an ideal course if you are going to work with a sports team or individual and you will need to be on hand to provide any necessary injury treatment.

It is worth searching online for local courses in your area as rates can fluctuate, but make sure that they are accredited and recognised by the HSE. If your clinic is located at another business it may be worth speaking to their office manager or health and safety officer as they may provide regular first aid training and refresher courses to their staff that you can also enrol on to, at a fraction of the usual cost.

Suggested websites to gauge types of courses available and their costs:

www.firstaidtraining.co.uk

www.redcrossfirstaidtraining.co.uk

www.sja.org.uk

Join your therapy's main affiliation (mine is the ISRM – Institute of Sport and Remedial Massage) and the CNHC – Complementary and Natural Healthcare Council, and any others recommended to you by your tutors. Subscribe to websites or online magazines (e.g. Massage World) that will keep you up-to-date – remember, you want to stay more informed than your clients and ahead of the competition!

It is vital that you attend CPDs throughout your career, both for the quality and diversity of your own practice and for affiliation requirements (roughly 15-20 points a year).

See ***Links and Resources*** *for further CPD website suggestions.*

CHAPTER 2

SETTING UP YOUR BUSINESS

CHOOSING YOUR PLACE OF WORK

This should be a careful consideration as once you have established yourself in a particular location it will be time-consuming and affect your income if you decide to move. This will also decide the type of clientele you will be targeting and attracting.

Working from home

The benefits of setting up at home are obvious – no travel time or expense incurred, convenient to you and there is no room rent to pay. You will also be able to off-set some of your related household expenses for tax purposes, such as phone lines, electricity etc. Hours are flexible, especially if you need to consider child-care.

The negatives are that you have strangers continually coming into your home and a comfortable, clean and tidy space needs to be constantly maintained for clients.

It can also be quite isolating as there is no other staff with whom to socialise and no-one to discuss or query issues that may arise regarding treatment advice.

If you live with others (adults or children), they need to be aware and compliant that you and your client are not to be disturbed – doors banging, children shouting and general house noise is not conducive to a relaxing environment - it may mean that you can only treat clients when everyone is out and this may restrict your earning potential.

Also consider how accessible your property is – does it have free parking or is it near a bus stop or station? People don't want to spend ages getting to you and then have to struggle home after a relaxing treatment.

Mobile work

The main benefit of mobile work – working at clients' homes or working with specific groups (e.g. dance troupe, sports teams, musicians), is that there are no overhead costs to consider except your own equipment. It will also be beneficial to have a car although I know a few therapists in

London who are quite happy travelling by public transport. This means carrying a heavy couch and bag around (I don't care how light the manufacturer says the "portable" couch is, at the end of a busy day it will feel like a ton!). Some therapists don't carry a couch but use the floor or client's furniture on which to treat but this will ultimately lead to back and shoulder problems for you so try to avoid doing this unless floor work is specific to your treatment.

If you are not working with a team or group then you need to find your own clients – this will usually mean some investment in advertising and marketing such as a website or an introductory letter to households in an area you would like to work. You should also try and establish some sort of referral service with other related services such as hairdressers, physiotherapists and holistic clinics (*see* ***Building Your Business*** *with further referral ideas*) – and encourage word of mouth – this is your best form of advertising - and the cheapest, too!

The negatives to mobile work is that if you spend too much time travelling from one client to the next, this will limit your number of clients treated in a day and you will have to add this cost to your treatment, making your service more expensive than a clinic-based one.

If travelling by car then the cost of petrol, parking and depreciation of the car will also have to be considered within the treatment cost.

A good way of making mobile work more cost-effective is to suggest to existing clients to bring two or three friends to their house and treating everyone in a block. This will cut down travel time, increase clients and make your time more efficient and financially rewarding.

A word of caution: *when visiting clients of the opposite sex, I would advise ensuring that their partner is also present so that nothing can be misconstrued and that your safety is never compromised. Many female therapists do not accept bookings from men if it is the first time they are meeting them – personally, I have only treated male partners of existing clients and made sure that they were there too, but I have refused work that requires my attendance at a hotel or house where there is no other person I trust present. Be aware of the risks and let your safety be the deciding factor, not the money.*

Working for Others

When first starting out as a massage therapist, you may choose to be employed by an established business. This is a good way of gaining experience and seeing how a therapy clinic is run without any financial risk to yourself.

The most typical employers of massage therapists tend to be beauty clinics or spas as more medically-based clinics tend to recruit on a self-employed basis.

The upside of being employed is that there is already an established clientele and you can benefit from other team members' experience and knowledge. You will also receive holiday/sick pay and income tax will be dealt with by your employer.

The downside is that the employer is in charge of your work hours and bookings so you may be working a long day with minimum breaks in order to meet the demands of the business.

However, this option is worth considering, and six months in such a business environment will give you good grounding and confidence to then take the next step of becoming self-employed.

Working for Yourself

Most individuals who train to become massage therapists are usually planning to become self-employed. Establishing and running a successful massage clinic requires hard work and dedication but the rewards and benefits of working for yourself cannot be underestimated.

Renting space

Many businesses are looking to increase income and will be happy to rent you space, especially as our line of work is not noisy or disruptive.

It is worth approaching some businesses to propose setting up a treatment room. The following are some suggestions:

- Hairdressers or beauty therapy clinics
- Sports/leisure/fitness facilities – private or public
- Physiotherapists/osteopaths/chiropractics
- Dentist/doctor surgeries
- Holistic/acupuncture clinics
- Large companies – some companies have a staff healthcare budget that you may become involved in e.g. the company pays you to treat their staff – back pain is the number one cause of work absence in this country - use this to your advantage!

Factors to consider when choosing space

Is there adequate room for a couch and for you to work around it without compromising your posture or inconveniencing the client?

I worked (for a brief period) in a small health clinic that provided dentistry and physiotherapy. My workspace was so small that I had to open the door when treating the client's legs and had to wheel the couch away from the wall to treat one side of their body!! Needless to say, I didn't stay there very long....

Does the room have a sink with hot and cold water?

> Apart from Environmental Health making this a requirement in most boroughs, running backwards and forwards to a sink that is at the end of a corridor is unhygienic, inconvenient and unprofessional.

How quiet is the area where the room is? Will you be disturbed by passing traffic or passers-by? How does the sound travel in the building?

> If your chosen massage is one that requires quiet and minimal interruptions, passing chatter or noise can be very disruptive to you and your client.

What is included within the rental charge? Heating, lighting, cleaning? Is there any equipment already in there and will they pay for any further equipment required or is that your outlay?

> All the above need to be considered and factored in to your outgoing costs.

Is there a reception service or will you need to manage your own calls, diary and bookings? Is there any kind of meet and greet service for clients who are enquiring or waiting to see you?

> At the end of a session the client usually wants to receive feedback on their treatment, re-book a session or discuss the treatment plan. Arriving clients often come early so these two periods may coincide - it is very helpful and useful if someone can greet the arrival while you deal with the previous client, otherwise a time slot may need to be factored in to prevent a client "clash". You will also need to set aside time during the day to deal with telephone enquiries – try not to leave a potential client waiting hours for a reply.

Who is responsible for any maintenance issues in the room such as lightbulbs, plumbing issues and heating/air-conditioning problems?

> The requirements of most treatment licences (*see* ***Licensing and Insuring***) are that you must provide proof that all the above are regularly checked and maintained.

Who else has access to the room? Will you need to have lockable cupboards to store record cards and sundries such as massage oil, couch roll etc?

> Record cards must be locked away (Data Protection Act 1998) and if you are sharing a room, you may need to give them access during treatment times or lock away your own equipment to prevent their use without your permission. You will also need to rely on the other therapist leaving the room in a good and clean condition for you.

Are there any time restrictions that will affect you? Does the business open and close at particular times/weekends that will affect when you can book clients?

> Ensure that you are aware of any holiday closures of the business from which you are renting. For example, they may close for the Easter weekend or for one or two weeks around the Christmas holidays - these can be busy times for the therapist and so you will be losing potential income but still paying the rent.

Will you be a key-holder or are you relying on others to open and close the building?

> Relying on others may result in them being late to open the premises and you standing on the doorstep with your client trying to find an emergency alternative location or, worse still, having to send that client home - unfortunately, this has happened although thankfully not frequently. You can avoid this by making sure your work day starts at least an hour after opening time or that you simply have a key.

The benefits of renting the space is that, after the rent has been paid, all the money you earn is yours – the more hours you put in, the more lucrative the returns will be.

The downside of this is that when times are slow or when the business is closed or you go away for a holiday, the rent will still need to be paid.

When negotiating the rent, suggest paying only 50% of the rent for the first month to give you time to build a clientele, 75% the second month and full rent from the third month onwards. Business owners are usually receptive to this as it indicates a knowledge of gradual client building and that you plan to be there for a while.

This is a great way to be independent and a master of your own time - you also reap the rewards of your hard work and this makes working extremely rewarding and enjoyable!

If you are just starting out and only have a few clients, it may be better to offer a percentage of your treatment to the business owner instead of rent. This is more common when working for a clinic – the split is often 50/50 but try not to agree to a 60/40 split (to them) for as you become busier, it can be demotivating to watch the results of your hard work go into someone else's pockets. If you see this happening, don't be afraid to renegotiate e.g. try and get a bigger percentage when you exceed a certain amount of treatments per month.

The following checklist will aid as a reminder of all the requirements that may need consideration when looking at a room for setting up your business:

Room Rental Checklist

- Size of room
- Any equipment included
- Lighting - dimmer switch?
- Controllable heating/ventilation
- Cleaning services/bin emptying
- Sink with hot/cold water (drinking water available?)
- Location of nearest toilets
- Storage space for supplies
- Lockable/secure cupboard/cabinet for record cards/valuable items
- Noise levels around room
- Phone lines (you may need this for internet/card payment facilities)
- Available Wi-Fi and mobile phone network coverage
- Nearest laundering facility
- **COST!!!!**

Basic equipment needed for therapy room

- Adjustable-height couch
- Couch covers
- Towels to cover client
- Face cradle (breathing holes in massage couches are not very comfortable)
- Adjustable stool for therapist
- Headrest/pillow and leg bolster (vinyl-covered will ensure a more hygienic clean)
- Massage medium – have at least two options such as lotion and oil - clients may have allergies to some ingredients
- disinfectant for hard surfaces and vinyl-covered bolsters/pillows
- lockable record box
- record cards
- writing material (you may wish to write after-care advice for your client to take away)

*See **Links and Resources** for suggested equipment websites*

Setting your hours and prices

Decide on how many hours you are prepared to work and what restrictions you may have, such as child care, study commitments etc. Be realistic and don't set yourself unreasonable or unattainable goals - you will spend your future years regretting it and working long hours trying to rectify it.

Decide on the income you require - is this your sole income or is it subsidising another source of earnings? Is there a partner who is contributing to the bills or are you the only earner? Work out your annual budget and how much you need to earn to pay bills and have some to spare for tax and savings. Divide this by approximately 48 weeks (allowing for national holidays, your holiday/sick days). You now have your weekly desired earnings.

Divide this, by how many hours you are prepared to work (not including breaks) to get your hourly rate. If the clinic already has a set charge, then you can work out how many clients you will need to treat to receive the desired total, excluding the percentage payable to the owner (don't forget that if you are doing mobile work you will have to cost in travelling time into your charge).

Here is an example:

Annual income required for cost of living: £25000 gross

Divide by 48 weeks (allowing for holidays): £520 per week needed

Hours available to work: 25 hours

520/25=£21

Outgoings to consider:

Room rental

Petrol

Consumables e.g. tissues, oils, record cards

These need to be taken into account and added to the cost of the treatment so that you are not working just to break even, or even worse, at a loss.

Bear in mind that if you are a sole trader (self-employed), approximately a third of your income must be set aside for tax and national insurance.

You will also get a good idea of hourly rates by checking out the local competition. Ring around or visit various clinics to get an idea of prices in the area – you don't want to be too cheap otherwise you will undervalue your product, but conversely, you don't want to price yourself out of the market.

If you are in an exclusive area or facility, your prices should reflect that – be aware of the demographics you are targeting and set your charges accordingly.

It is up to you whether you offer a treatment package - many clinics/ individuals offer a price reduction if a certain amount of treatments are purchased (e.g. buy 10, get the 11th free). If you do this it is advisable to stipulate a "use by" date (I suggest 6-12 months), as otherwise the course can get dragged out for several years by which time your prices may have increased or you may have even changed location!

Give these decisions careful consideration as the output and income of your business rests on the accuracy of these calculations.

CHAPTER 3

LICENSING AND INSURANCE

It is a legal requirement and good professional practice to take out comprehensive insurance cover even if you work from home:

- Medical Malpractice which covers treatment risk
- Personal/Professional Indemnity which covers advice you give that may affect someone financially
- Public Liability which covers if someone slips and injures themselves on your premises
- Product Liability covers a defect in any product sold

Most insurance companies will offer a package that covers all the above, including free legal advice.

Balens Limited is the company I use and they are very familiar with all types of therapy and treatments: www.balens.co.uk

You will need to contact your local council, normally the Environmental Health department, to check whether you need a Personal Special Treatments Licence to carry out massage. Some authorities just ask for proof that you belong to particular affiliations and no further licensing is required. Others will charge a fee for a licence that lasts from one to five years, which allows you to massage clients within the licensing borough.

The facility from where you massage also requires a Special Treatments Licence and a representative from the local authority will visit your place of work and charge you accordingly, normally per room. If you are leasing from another individual, this will usually be their responsibility but always check that everything is legal and above board.

The following is an example taken from a couple of London borough websites detailing requirements (explanations are mine) that need to be met before a Special Treatments Licence is granted, but always check with your own borough for specific details:

Example of a borough council's requirements for a Special Treatments Licence:

Terms of Licence

- Licences are granted for a specific length of time e.g. 12 months to three years)

Displaying the Licence

- The licence needs to be displayed in a prominent position, visible to the public

Opening Times

- Opening and closing times need to be prominently displayed

Price List/Tariff

- A price list of all treatments offered (inc VAT) must be displayed prominently within the premises

Criminal History

- You have a duty to inform the council of any criminal convictions obtained during the licensing period

Insurance

- Employers liability; Public Liability; Professional/Personal Indemnity

Control of Waste

- How and when rubbish is removed

Structure and Cleanliness

- All areas in room and equipment to be kept clean and maintained in good repair and condition
- Handwash stations/shower facilities must be provided for hygienic washing/drying
- Animals not permitted in rooms (unless service dogs). This may vary council to council

Electrical Safety

- Any plugged appliances (e.g. lamps, steriliser, fan/heater), must be tested annually to receive a PAT (Portable Appliance Test) certificate

Fire Safety

- Awareness of means of escape from building with signs/emergency lighting as appropriate

WC Facilities

- Kept clean and in good order
- Washing facilities with hot and cold running water, soap and paper towels/hand-dryer
- Ventilated space between treatment room and toilets

Sinks/Showers

- Ensure these are cleaned regularly
- Ventilation
- Sufficient natural or mechanical ventilation

Lighting

- Adequate and suitable – from a therapist's point of view, dimmable lights are ideal as bright tube lighting can be blinding when lying directly underneath it

Heating

- Sufficient heating maintained throughout premises. Clients usually have to undress to some degree, so a warm room in cold weather is a necessity

Infection control

- If using equipment, it needs to be decontaminated and sterilised between treatments

Personal Hygiene

- Hands kept clean and washed before and after treatment. High degree of personal cleanliness and wear suitable, clean and appropriate clothing
- You should not treat clients if you have any known, or likely to be a carrier of, a disease likely to be transmitted during treatment
- Any open sores, cuts, boils or open wounds on practitioners must be effectively covered with waterproof, impermeable dressing
- Practitioner does not smoke or consume food or drink during course of treatment

Record Keeping

- Client records should have the following information about the client:
    - o Name and address
    - o Type of treatment given

- o Name of Practitioner
- o Date treatment was given
- o Assessment of any contra-indications
- o Informed consent of the client
- o After-care advice - written or verbal
- o Age of client (anyone under the age of 16 must be accompanied by a parent or guardian and the client record signed by parent/ guardian)

Contra-indications which must be considered:

- Eczema
- Psoriasis
- Haemophilia
- Heart disorders
- High/low blood pressure
- Epilepsy
- Diabetes
- Allergies

And establish whether client is:

- taking medication or blood-thinning agents
- breast-feeding
- pregnant

If your premises do not meet all the above requirements after an inspection by a council representative, you will usually be issued a warning with a date by which you will need to comply with the recommendations. Preparation and knowledge will avoid any delays in obtaining your licence.

CHAPTER 4

BUILDING YOUR BUSINESS

THE BUSINESS PLAN

Writing a business plan is good practice even if you won't be using it to approach banks or investors. A good plan helps to clarify your business idea, spot potential problems, set out your goals and measure your progress.

You will need a business plan if you want to secure an investment or a loan from a bank. It can also help to convince suppliers and potential employees to support you. It does not have to be complicated and helps to define your long-term objectives.

The following breakdown of the plan is an aid to set out and ensure that all areas required of a plan are covered.

1. Executive Summary

This outlines your business proposal. It is usually written last but needs to go on the first page of the plan. It will be read by people who are unfamiliar with your industry so avoid jargon.

The summary highlights the most important points and should sum up the following areas:

- Your service and its advantages
- Your opportunity in the market
- Your track record to date
- Financial projections
- Funding requirements and expected returns

2. The Business

Explain the background to your business including:

- The length of time you have been developing the idea
- Work carried out to date

- Any related experience to date
- The proposed ownership structure of the business
- Explain what your service is and any weak points it may have

3. Markets and Competitors

- Focus on the segments of the market you plan to target e.g. local customers, office workers, and particular age group
- Indicate whether the market segment is growing/declining
- Important trends and reasons behind them
- Key characteristics of customers (age, sex, income)
- Any competitors and why customers will come to you instead of them
- Show how you understand competitors' reactions to losing business and demonstrate how you will respond to it

4. Sales and Marketing

- How your service will meet your customers' specific needs
- Show how your price and quality of service will compare with competitors
- Show how you will identify and reach potential customers
- Demonstrate that you have a clearly defined pool of potential customers
- Show how you will promote your service

5. Management

- People reading the business plan need to be given an idea of why they should have faith in the management of your set-up
- Show your strengths and outline how you will cope with any weaknesses
- Describe background and experience of each team member

- Outline procedures for management of accounts, sales and stock control, if relevant
- Demonstrate your commitment to the business, showing how much time and money you will contribute and what your salary will be

6. Operations

- What facilities the business will have and how it will deliver the service to the customer
- Pros and cons of location
- What equipment will be needed

7. Financial Forecasts

- A realistic sales forecast which shows cash flow - how much money you expect to be flowing in and out of your bank account. You must show that your business will have access to enough money to survive
- The forecast also needs to show Profit and Loss – how the business will move forward and forecast the annual profit and loss for each of the first two or three years of trading

8. Financial Requirements

- How much finance you will want and in what form (overdraft/loan) and state what the finance will be used for
- Confirm that you will be able to afford it

9. Assessing the Risks

- Look at the business plan and isolate areas where something could go wrong and what you would do if it actually happens
- Consider a range of "what-if" scenarios and if cash flow is severely affected, how you will respond to rectify this
- Assessing the risks will help to minimise problems and build up your credibility with any investor/banker

10. Appendices

- Detailed financial forecasts and any other relevant information such as market research data, target customers

11. Presenting the Plan

- Keep your plan short - focus on what the reader needs to know
- Make it professional - put a cover on the plan and title it. Include a contents page
- Test it – re-read it yourself – show the plan to friends and experts and ask for feedback

You can download business plan templates from the Princes Trust website www.princes-trust.org.uk and you can read examples of different business plans at www.bplans.co.uk

CARDS AND LEAFLETS

There are entire books, websites and expensive courses geared to marketing your business (and which I will leave to the experts), but there are other effective ways of attracting clients without having to spend large amounts of money before you have even established your business.

The first thing to do is to print some business cards. Have your name, relevant qualification, address of business and contact details e.g. mobile, email etc.

I suggest you also use the flip-side of the card otherwise it is wasted advertising space. You could list the types of massage you offer or the health conditions you typically treat – my own card has date/time columns on which I can write appointments.

Ensure the size of the card is credit card-sized so that it can fit into wallet slots otherwise it will end up at the bottom of a bag or battered in a pocket!

You may also like to consider having leaflets printed with more detailed information about your treatments offered and associated prices. Keep the information clear and simple and don't bombard the reader with too much technical/medical detail. Leaflet dropping to houses and businesses tends not to be very cost-effective. Face-to face introductions are much more productive and then leaflets can be left as a reinforcement and reminder of your services.

If you are a mobile worker or working from home, the leaflets may not be particularly useful but if you are renting a room within a building, displaying them in a prominent position will be invaluable.

REFERRALS

The best form of advertising is word-of-mouth, especially in our industry. Someone may look good on paper but their hands-on work may be ineffective. You need to get people talking about you and your treatments so try offering "taster" sessions to staff within your work facility. Contact local healthcare professionals, hairdressers and personal trainers as they are all great for spreading the word – they have good conversational relationships with their clients, and their clients usually trust their judgment on other services. Offer these professionals discounted or free treatments for referrals and try and send your clients their way when needed.

Word of advice: if you are referring a clinic or salon or individual to a client, you should have first-hand knowledge of their service. For example, I only recommend physiotherapists and osteopaths from whom I have received treatment.

You can also encourage existing clients to recommend you by giving them discount vouchers for the initial introductory treatment to pass on to family, friends or co-workers.

You can also offer an incentive to your existing clients by giving them a discount on their next treatment if someone they recommend books a treatment with you.

Contacting local groups or clubs and offering them a special rate or a free taster afternoon will help to build clientele, either at a clinic or in a home environment. You could offer a discount if several people book and meet at a venue; this could be a clubhouse or an individual's home – the time you save treating several people at one place will cover any discount you may offer.

The big plus of our service is that it is enjoyable and a treat (some clients even view it as a necessity) and so it's not a difficult treatment to sell.

Whatever you decide to do, don't sit at home or in your treatment room waiting for the phone to ring - get out there and contact people and let them know what an effective and beneficial service you are offering!

CHAPTER 5

PROVIDING EXCELLENT CUSTOMER CARE

COMMUNICATION

When a potential client calls to make initial contact and enquire about your treatment, give them an outline but don't overload them with detail. Try to discourage the caller from giving you their complete medical history or describing every ache and pain in detail. Ensure you ask specific questions to filter the information you may need.

Avoid giving advice over the phone – especially if you haven't met the client yet – as you don't want to encourage a free "helpline".

Avoid making promises or setting unrealistic expectations of what results you might get with your treatment. Even if you give a great treatment, if you fail to meet the client's expectations or your "predicted" outcome, you will have under-delivered in the client's eyes.

When taking the booking, always take the client's name and contact number and possibly email. Repeat the booking day, time and duration of treatment back to the client and let them know what payment methods you are able to accept.

Ensure they know where your location is and inform them of any parking/travel issues that may arise (e.g. parking meters that are only an hour's stay). If you are going to the client's house, find out what the parking arrangements are or how close they are to public transport, if that is your choice of travel.

Try to confirm the booking by text or email so that the client has a visual reference of the booking. I like to send a reminder the day before the treatment as it is common for people to forget they have a booking or get the day or time wrong. This will minimise the "no-shows" which result in loss of income and a missed opportunity for rebooking with another client.

If it is the client's first booking with you, stipulate any cancellation policy you may have at this time. It is usual to charge a percentage or total of the treatment cost due to loss of potential earnings. This is difficult to implement if you have never met the person before but much easier once you know them!

As you become busier, you will have clients who are on "stand-by" for any last-minute cancellations. This waiting list is very useful as you can fill slots straight away and also avoid charging a fee to the client who has just cancelled.

Try to meet and greet your client on the day rather than getting someone to direct them to you – the personal touches are always appreciated. Ask if they need to use the bathroom - often they have been travelling and only realise they need to "go" once they are undressed and on the couch - save yourself some time by thinking ahead.

THE CONSULTATION

The consultation is very important for setting the relationship between you and the client. This is where you find out the client's expectations and how to best manage them. It is also the time when the client is assessing you, your professionalism and whether they think you can help them or not.

It is best to have a record card or screen with specific questions so that you can control what information is extracted and that you don't miss out anything that could be relevant.

Below is an example of the headings I use when consulting with a client for the first time, but check with your local council for legal requirements (*see* ***Licensing and Insurance*** *– record keeping*)

- Name
- Address
- Contact details – phone/email
- Date of Birth
- Occupation (this gives you an idea of how their work may affect their body)

- Medication – any long-term or short-term medications, health issues and any side-effects this may cause (you can ask the client, you're not expected to recognise all medications)
- Previous Medical History - find out if the client has had any major operations (this will include caesareans), bone breaks, severe soft tissue tears etc.
- Sport & Exercise – how active are they? Does the activity cause the problem or can it be used to rectify any outstanding issues?
- Sleep – poor or disturbed sleep may indicate pain or stress and tiredness can lead to more injury and reduced tissue repair
- AOI (any other information) – the above topics may reveal any further issues you may need to note, such as migraines, teeth grinding, chronic pain that the client has just become accustomed to, etc.
- Client Consent – the client must consent to treatment so a written and signed consent is the easiest way to do this. If the client is under 16 the parent or guardian of that child must sign a written consent for treatment, and must stay in the room as a chaperone during treatment.

Records must be kept on the premises and available for inspection for two years (this length of time may vary but check with your council).

At this point, I then do a postural assessment to see what the body is doing in a stationary position and in movement, but that is the therapist's individual choice.

You should have a good idea of what the client's issues are but what may sound like a major problem to you may not be what the client is coming to see you for. Ask them to prioritise what issues they would like you to address but be realistic about how you think you can help them. People appreciate honesty and you need to manage their expectations and possible outcomes. For example, someone who has had chronic neck and back pain for six months is not going to be completely pain-free after one or even two sessions, and it is best to point this out and suggest a treatment plan that may give better results.

If you do not believe that your treatment will be of any benefit to the client, refer them on to another therapist. You are not a miracle worker and will not be able to treat anyone and everything - leave your ego at the door and don't blow your own trumpet about what you can achieve - no-one likes or trusts boastfulness! Your client will appreciate your candour and be more likely to return to you for a more relevant issue.

During treatment I recommend that you outline which areas you will be working on. This prevents a misunderstanding of which areas will be treated as some clients assume that the whole body will be massaged, whereas various types of massage just concentrate on particular areas. Some clients also remember an area of the body that has been niggling and may ask you to include it within the treatment time – you can either factor this in to the treatment or note it down for the subsequent sessions.

After the treatment is complete, clients like to have feedback about the treatment and how you think the client might be able to improve the issue. You may like to offer strengthening exercises or stretching movements that you think may benefit the individual. Always demonstrate the movement and then teach it to the client – executing the movement correctly will help them remember it – but allow for that within the treatment time. After the session, record the date and treatment given as this is a legal requirement, but also aids planning of any follow-up treatments.

Record-taking tip

One of my first jobs was working at a physiotherapy clinic in Clapham and all therapists had to record all treatment on their record cards. The layout was clear and informative and I have always adopted this method (**SOAP**) ever since.

- **S**ubjective observations of the client - e.g. frequent headaches, painful right knee, neck pain

- **O**bjective observations of the therapist - e.g. scoliosis, uneven hip line, hypertonic trapezius
- **A**ction during treatment - e.g. myofascial release to hypertonic muscles, active stretching to spine, lateral work to the hips
- **P**lan of action – this could be exercises given to the client, recommendations made to the client, what areas need to be addressed in the next session.

Whilst we're on the subject of time-keeping, you need to allocate time into the session for undressing, dressing (you will need longer in winter than summer!), and any feedback or suggested home treatment plan. This will take a little practise and you may run over several times before you get the timings right – try and factor in a 15 minute gap after new clients to allow for running over. Once you start booking back-to-back clients, you will not have this flexibility and leaving a client waiting is very poor service, unprofessional and needs to be avoided at all costs.

Re-book the client before they leave, but if they prefer to call you, offer to send them a reminder to prompt a re-booking.

If the client was in pain or nervous about the effects of treatment, it's good customer service to give them a follow-up call in the following day or two to see how they are feeling and how they responded to your treatment.

A good first treatment will nearly always lead to a repeat booking or a referral so always conduct a thorough consultation and you will reap the rewards in the long-term.

The following is an example of the front and back of a record card. You can opt to have these printed or hand-write them yourself. These examples are just for guidance and the final layout will be your choice.

CLIENT RECORD CARD Side 1:

Client Record		
Name:		**Tel/Mobile:**
Address:		
D.O.B:		
MEDS/CONTRAS		
PMH:		
Sport/Ex:		
Sleep:		
AOI:		
Reasons for Visit:		
Client Consent:	I confirm I fully understand the treatment and its benefits, and my questions have been answered to my satisfaction	**Signed:**

Client Record Card Side 2:

Date:	
S **O** **A** **P**	
Date:	
S **O** **A** **P**	
Date:	
S **O** **A** **P**	
Date:	
S **O** **A** **P**	

HOW TO KEEP CLIENTS

Therapist/Client relationship

During treatment allow the client to set the pace of conversation. Some people like silence and will not appreciate the therapist chatting away throughout treatment, whereas some individuals love to talk and will be happy to converse for the duration.

There are some personalities that are very excitable and give out a lot of nervous energy - slow your conversation down so that it calms them as it is difficult to give any type of massage with a "wired" client.

Over a period of time, you may build a relationship with the client. The client may reveal personal information to you that is not connected to the treatment and this must remain private between you and the client. Don't discuss clients' personal information with other clients - they will realise that you are not discreet and cannot be trusted to maintain their privacy.

Try not to encourage excessive emotional intimacy with clients – this can be very wearing and draining on you as the therapist, and for which you are not qualified to cope with. Be supportive but don't get pulled in to the individual's drama.

Avoid talking about yourself too much – the client looks forward to this time they have to themselves and the massage may be a rare opportunity to have "me" time – not "you" time! Try not to moan or complain about work, colleagues or money – this can be awkward and unprofessional and can make the client feel uncomfortable.

Clients may also tell you about their family, friends and children. They may also let you know when an important event is coming up, such as birthdays, sporting event, even an operation date – make a note of this information so that you can follow it up at another session, or even send them a text to let them know you have remembered the event. Showing a genuine interest in the client goes a long way and makes the client feel special – which, of course, they are!

RETENTION

It is easier to keep an existing client than to try and find a new one. Make sure your client feels valued and appreciated by your actions. This may vary according to the individual client but making this effort is invaluable to you as a therapist. The following are ideas on how to make this happen.

Send a reminder the day before your client's appointment. This reduces the possibility of a client forgetting the appointment or realising they have a diary clash. Last-minute cancellations and clients who just fail to turn up ("no-shows"), are the bane of the therapist's work life, and steps should always be taken to avoid this.

If a client chooses not to re-book their next session due to workload or holiday disruptions, offer to send them a reminder at the appropriate time – it is easier to respond to a text, email or phone call, than to initiate the call in the first place. Put a note in your diary so that you don't forget to do this.

As previously mentioned, if a client has been nervous or anxious about having a treatment of a particular issue, it's always good practice to follow up with a call, text or email to see how their body has responded. This is excellent customer service and lets the client know you have their well-being in mind.

Some clients have difficulty booking in advance and are always looking for the last minute treatment. Make a note of these clients and if you don't have a waiting list, call them with any cancellations – they will appreciate that you thought of them.

One of my clients runs several businesses and also has many family demands made upon her so finds it difficult to book ahead. If I get any cancellations on the day, I will always text her to let her know and 80% of the time she takes them!

Endeavour not to cancel clients or move their bookings around too much - they are your priority so only change their bookings in an emergency or for a one-off situation. Having said that, some clients are more flexible than others and once you have established a good relationship, these clients will be able to help you juggle your diary.

Plan your own holidays and days off in advance so clients can plan their treatment slots around your absence. If you are going away for a period of time, you may want to refer them to another local therapist, just in case they have an emergency.

Be true to your word – if you say you are going to research something for a client, source a product for them, write an exercise prescription, lend them a book - then DO IT!

DEALING WITH DIFFICULT CLIENTS

Rarely, you may come across a client who, for a variety of possible reasons, you may want to discourage from booking with you.

The treatment-dependent client

This type of client normally has a condition that has no specific diagnosis and spends a lot of time and money visiting a myriad of different therapists, usually with little or no improvement in their health. The issue with this type of client is that when they have so many different treatments and therapists, if there is an improvement, the client will be unsure which one has been the most effective and will want to continue with all of them, "just in case" they jettison the wrong one. There is also a possibility that the condition they have is being over-treated by so many various techniques that the treatments are aggravating the condition, rather than improving it. Professionally, if you feel certain types of treatments are inhibiting the client's improvement, you must deal with this carefully. It is never a good idea to dismiss another therapist/treatment as unnecessary as this may affect your reputation with that therapist. Also, the client may view this advice as unwelcome as they have become dependent on that therapy. Be professional and considerate when discussing a future treatment plan with the client and, if possible, and with the client's consent, contact the other therapist/s to discuss the case. Try and agree with the therapists the best way to move forward for the benefit of the client, bearing in mind that there will probably be a considerable amount of emotional and psychological factors affecting this individual.

Whilst I was working at a multi-disciplinary clinic, I had a regular weekly client who complained of a multitude of non-specific painful areas (he would start from his head and work down to his feet, pointing out areas that he wanted me to have a look at). He always felt better after treatment but overall, the condition was not improving. At the same time he was being treated by an osteopath and a physiotherapist, with similar results. Eventually, with his permission, we called a meeting between all three therapists to discuss his case, with a view to reduce his treatments. We then presented our conclusions and recommendations to the client who was happy to comply as we were all then working in unison and he felt that we had his best interests at heart. Eventually this client was able to reduce all his treatments and now only visits for the odd maintenance tweaking!

The "flaky" client

This type of client is someone who regularly cancels or forgets their treatment continuously. Point out any cancellation or no-show charges you may have (these need to be printed somewhere or within a text or email that they have previously received), and attempt to recoup your losses. Unfortunately, this kind of client rarely "gets it" that you have lost potential income and that your time has value, and is often unhappy about being charged. A suggested way to get round this is to take advance payment on the understanding that if they do not turn up for their appointment or cancel with insufficient notice, they will forfeit that payment. This usually sorts out the genuine clients from the time-wasters. These individuals are more work than they are worth so let them go!

The "pervy" client

Unfortunately massage can still carry a seedy implication and subsequently can sometimes attract unwanted individuals. These individuals are easy to get rid of over the phone but if they make it into your treatment room they may make sexual comments or advances. Ask them to leave as soon as you feel uncomfortable or suggest they look elsewhere for a treatment. Never put your safety at risk and it is better to lose the money than work through a very uncomfortable session. Thankfully this doesn't happen often but be prepared with an assertive statement if it ever does such as "I believe you have misunderstood the service I provide and your behaviour is making me feel uncomfortable. I will now end the session and ask that you get dressed and leave".

Clients with personal hygiene issues

Some clients may have consistent body odour issues. If you are uncomfortable dealing with the problem head on it may be easier to suggest/ encourage the client to shower before seeing you. Sometimes this isn't possible but if you know a client is going to work out first or comes to you on a bicycle, it can be difficult working on sweating skin, especially in hot weather. It may be useful to have some deodorising wipes available to clients to help them freshen up.

Clothing

Often clients will ask what to wear to a session - as I do postural assessments, some people are uncomfortable standing in their underwear so always give the client an idea of what you will be doing in the body analysis so they can make an informed choice about their comfort. For example, I ask men to either wear gym shorts that can be rolled up or close-fitting underpants, as cotton boxer shorts can "gap" in awkward places. Minimise embarrassment and make your clients feel as comfortable as possible.

PERSONAL HEALTH AND HYGIENE

You and your environment

It may seem this goes without saying so apologies if I'm stating the obvious, but in my time of receiving treatment from various therapists and from listening to horror stories from my clients, I have compiled the following list of "considerations".

- Have a clean body - don't massage straight after a workout or rush out of the house without showering
- Wash your hands before and after EVERY client – after massaging, your hands are covered in your client's skin cells, even if not visible to the eye
- If you have any cuts or open wounds they must be covered with a waterproof dressing. I have found that plasters fall off within the treatment due to oils/lotions and now use non-latex surgical gloves which clients say feels just like bare skin
- Change your top every day - if the weather is very hot, you may need to change during the day as well
- Keep your breath fresh - if you've eaten before a session, check teeth for food debris and pop in a breath freshener!
- Don't wear any heavy scents in perfume, aftershave or even spray deodorants - the wearer never smells it as much as the person smelling it. A strong perfumed smell is off-putting and constantly irritates the senses if your client is trying to relax.
- Keep nails short, unpainted and clean – your hands are your tools, not your fashion accessory and will look much more professional (unless you're a manicurist!!)
- Don't turn up to work with a hangover (from alcohol or drugs). This will always reflect negatively on you, no matter what your client says outwardly to you. Your work is aimed at promoting and encouraging well-being so you need to practise what you preach.

- Look after your physical fitness - having a good level of endurance and core strength will mean that you minimise fatigue and stop you feeling "burnt out" after a busy day or week. Eat regularly and healthily – you should be leading by example

Your room

- Keep your room clean and dust-free. Even if there are cleaners employed in the facility always double-check this as they often cut corners.

- Change couch roll tissue after every client.

- Have plenty of clean towels available and change bedding regularly.

- Keep the room comfortably warm but well-ventilated. During winter, I have a small electric blanket that can be switched on to warm up freezing clients which goes down very well!

- Lie on your treatment couch to see what your client sees – check for dusty skirting boards, cobwebs on the ceiling, bright lights shining in the eyes, dirty cupboards and shelves and stained floor - if you can see it, so can your client.

Job Satisfaction

Providing a high standard of treatment will not only be appreciated by your clients, but will also give you intrinsic job satisfaction. Knowing that you are delivering the best possible service is very satisfying and motivates you to learn more and do better.

Aim to achieve your financial goals - and possibly surpass them. All that hard work can definitely pay off. Keep focussed and look after your clients.

Enjoy the time with your clients. It's a great opportunity to meet a diverse group of people with whom to chat and discuss an infinite amount of topics. I am constantly entertained, impressed, horrified and intrigued by the multitude of stories that people have been kind enough to impart to me - I have learnt and continue to learn from my clients!

CHAPTER 6

RUNNING YOUR BUSINESS

TYPICAL WORK DAY

Once you have started treating clients regularly, you will set your own work day rhythm but it may be useful and insightful to show you my typical day:

- 8am: I message clients booked for the following day with a reminder of their appointment time
- I respond to any messages received either late the night before or early that morning. Double-check start time for that day
- 9:30-9:45am: I arrive early at work to prepare for the day. This consists of ensuring I have enough clean towels and that the room has been cleaned adequately by the night cleaners i.e. bin emptied, floor swept and surfaces, inc sink, wiped down
- Find the record cards for the day's client list and have a quick read-through
- Prepare cards for any new client assessments that may be booked in
- Put phone to silent and "treatment in progress" sign on the door
- 10am: Meet client at reception and escort them to treatment room
- Get relevant updates from client regarding their well-being. Many of my clients are comfortable undressing in front of me whilst doing this, but if not, I pop out of the room to give them a couple of minutes to get comfortable on the couch
- Treat client – I often give feedback and advice during treatment to avoid too much conversation at the end of the treatment time as this is when it is easy to run late
- 10:55: I leave the client to get dressed (I tell them that I will return in a couple of minutes - this stops them from taking ages to get up and dressed!) and I use that time to write up client notes

- 10:57: I come back to the treatment room, give any further advice/exercises, re-book the client and take payment. File the completed record card.
- 11am: meet the next client at reception
- 12pm: I treat a maximum of three clients back-to-back (i.e. no breaks in between) although I prefer to do less
- 1pm: Lunch – catch up with any missed calls or texts from clients
- 2-4pm: clients
- 4pm: Break - respond to any clients' messages
- 4:30-7pm: clients
- 7pm – end of day. Tidy room and store record cards in lockable box/cupboard

I try to schedule in a morning break but sometimes that's not feasible, so I work through until lunch-time (usually 1 or 2pm). I try to always schedule an hour for lunch. This gives me enough time to eat without rushing, read, rest and unwind before the afternoon session begins. I also respond to messages that I have received in the morning.

I normally work until 7pm but will definitely have an afternoon break (around 430/5pm). I try not to work more than three hours back-to-back as anything more leaves me pretty fatigued, but this differs for every-body.

End of day: I lock away my record cards in a cupboard in the room and tidy up the room - I try not to leave a messy room e.g. no couch cover, equipment left out, as fate usually conspires to make you late the next day and you have minimal time to prepare before the first client is hot on your heels!

Tips to make life easier

When you first start out, give yourself more frequent breaks until you are comfortable with the timings of your treatment. It is unprofessional to keep your client waiting, and if you don't respect your client's time, they will not respect yours. Never assume that if you are running late they can stay longer for you to make up the lost time, as often clients have to rush off to other appointments or their meter is about to run out!

Most clients are aware that they need to be out of the room as another client is waiting, but there are a few who, no matter what you say, want to sit around and talk or take an age to get dressed. I usually finish the treatment a few minutes earlier than usual to factor this in or try and book them with a break straight after so that it doesn't matter too much if they make you late.

If a client arrives late I will still finish at the appointed end time as I feel it is unfair to keep my next client waiting due to the tardiness of the first.

If I am late (thankfully very rarely!), and I have someone booked straight after, if the client agrees, I will give them a discount on their treatment and still finish at the appointed time. If I have time afterwards and the client is not in a rush, I will work into the break. Either way, the client is hopefully placated and I lose out in either time or money –which is a strong motivator to be on time.

Some treatment rooms have phones that link to reception. Early on in my practice I removed this phone as reception would call me to let me know my next client had arrived. This nearly always coincided at the point of the most relaxing or calming section of my treatment and the interruption was always unwelcome. However, this means that I have to be extremely punctual meeting my next client so that the reception staff are confident that I will show up on time and they are not left dealing with an irritable client who is missing valuable treatment time. I have found that when a client knows you are punctual and reliable, they will endeavour to be so too.

I also ask staff to keep my next client at reception rather than let them come straight to my room. I can be finishing with the previous client or tidying my room and I like to have a quick breather before the next massage. Do what works best for you.

ADMINISTRATION AND RECORD-KEEPING

As previously mentioned, clients' record cards must be kept somewhere safe and secure (lockable). Be aware that clients have the right to access their own records, if requested (*Data Protection Act 1998 part II*).

You must keep client records safe and in good condition for eight years from the date of the client's last visit to you, or if the client is a child, until his or her 25th birthday, or 26th birthday if the client was 17 when the treatment ended. If you close down your practice, you must arrange for safe storage of records and clients must be made aware of how to obtain their records if needed. Alternatively, you could return the record directly to the client if you have the opportunity to do so.

You must also keep the last two years of client records on the premises in the event of an inspection by Environmental Health as part of your treatment licence requirements.

Keep your client records up-to-date and every year I suggest you archive clients that you haven't treated in at least a year (but store them on the premises). Efficient house-keeping of records is good practice and will allow you to access old records easily, if necessary.

Book-keeping

I always attend to financial matters from home. I bank every couple of days and check my account daily.

I do my book-keeping weekly. This gives me greater control over what is going in and out and I avoid having to spend hours clearing a backlog of previously accumulated work.

Save all your receipts and keep a record of spending if you order online. Try to always have some sort of paper trail for money going in and out of your account in relation to your business.

When I was first self-employed as a beauty therapist, I kept putting off book-keeping from week to week. Eventually I had to tackle a couple of months' worth of accumulated receipts and records that would take me hours to clear. Some therapists I know leave all book-keeping to just before they have to submit accounts to HMRC which is extremely time-consuming and stressful. The more organised your account keeping, the less your accountant will have to do and the cheaper their bill to you will be!

If you are self-employed and do not have complicated accounting and tax issues, it is worth considering submitting your own accounts and saving annual accountants' fees. Check out advice and guidance online *www.hmrc.gov.uk/index.htm*

DEALING WITH QUIET TIMES

Sometimes during the work year, client demand slows down considerably. This can be caused by various factors such as a general decline due to the current financial climate, annual holidays when a large percentage of your clients may be away, lack of personal finances etc.

First thing is try not to panic! If it's just a week or two that is quiet, hold tight, work usually picks up when you least expect it. If it has been over several weeks, going into months, you need to take action.

Try messaging existing clients to prompt them into re-booking with you. Often clients have the intention of contacting you but life gets in the way and they don't get around to it.

Contact other health professionals local to you – offer them an incentive to recommending you to their clients (free/discounted massage).

Ensure that you are doing everything right and that clients are not staying away because of treatment dissatisfaction. Speak to reception if available to find out if there has been any negative client feedback and address any issues that may arise from this. If you have a good relationship with a few of your clients, ask them what you could do to improve your treatment or service generally and accept feedback generously and with an open mind.

If you work in or near a big office or business, try offering a treatment package to staff of that business - don't discount too heavily though as you want clients to value your work and not get used to having cheap sessions.

Send a discount voucher to your client together with a referral voucher for a friend – this benefits your existing client and you may gain a new client.

For the first and second Christmases of my business I sent a £5 voucher for an hour's massage to all my existing and past clients (but not more than a year since their last treatment) and an additional voucher for a recommended friend. Both vouchers needed to be used by the end of February to give some urgency to the offer. This worked very well as nearly all the existing and past clients used their vouchers, I gained several new clients and the usually quiet post-Christmas period was busy.

A great piece of advice that was given to me by a highly successful physiotherapist said that if I maintained a steady work-flow through August, when a large percentage of people go away for their holidays, the rest of the year would be fine –and he was right!

Eventually when your business has settled into a good rhythm, you may see a pattern emerging of busy versus quiet periods and you can plan your months accordingly. Quiet times are a good time for you to take some time off or offer seasonal promotions. Hopefully the busy periods will mean that you can take it a little bit easier and enjoy the quiet days without worrying.

PRICE INCREASES

Over a period of time, you may need or wish to increase your treatment prices. Several issues may influence this decision, the obvious one being that your basic overheads have increased, whether it be room rent, products or other general outgoings.

Another reason may be that other clinics around you have all increased their prices, making your charges appear too cheap. It's important to stay competitive but without alienating your existing and potential clientele.

If you are extremely busy and wish to reduce your hours or work-rate, increasing your treatment prices will create a natural drop-off of clients who are unable to afford your service or who have to reduce the frequency with which they visit you. Some therapists get around this problem by charging the existing clients the old rate and only charging new clients the increased rate.

Consider the amount by which you are increasing the price as it needs to be reasonable and competitive for your area and reflect any inflation rise. I always research several successful clinics in my work area to get an idea of the hourly rate that businesses are charging and what the public expect to pay. I usually increase by approximately 10% of the original cost, every two years – although whilst we had the double-dip recession, I didn't increase my prices at all. Clients were aware of the price freeze and were happy and receptive to an increase thereafter.

I also write a letter to existing clients, giving at least a month's notice of any upcoming increase. I include examples of local clinics so that clients know that they are still receiving value for money and that the increase is reasonable and well-considered.

Be aware that frequent price increases not directly responding to rent or rates increments may alienate clients who may feel that you are exploiting them or just getting greedy.

On the flip-side, not increasing your prices will indicate to clients that you are nervous of changing prices, possibly indicating lack of self-confidence in your service. Severely undercutting all the other local therapists to you will have a negative response from these businesses as you are devaluing both their, and your, service. This may not be important to you but remember that your professional reputation can be harmed by negative talk. Also be aware that good therapists are happy to recommend other therapists if they are unable to accommodate a client's request for treatment and that they would be less likely to do so if there is a large discrepancy between their charges and yours.

BUILDING A PROFESSIONAL NETWORK

The work life of a therapist can be quite isolated - especially if you decide to work from home or house visit only. Sometimes it can be useful and helpful if you have other colleagues, even if they are from different disciplines, off whom to bounce ideas. You may also need to refer your client on to a different therapy in order to facilitate their improvement.

The easiest and most effective way of doing this is to introduce yourself to other therapists in your area, preferably as a client/patient of that therapist. You should always recommend another therapist based on your own experience and opinion, and likewise, offer that therapist a free treatment so they can refer their patients to you. I would also include people of your own discipline in this list – it's always a good idea to receive a treatment of the same therapy as yours as a reminder of what your clients experience when they see you. It can also be useful to have another person to recommend your clients to if you are going away on holiday, off sick or just fully booked.

Build up your contact list with as diverse a selection as possible – you never know when you or your clients may need them!

MANAGING YOUR TIME OFF

Most employed people look at the self-employed and think that life must be really easy – taking time off when you want to, only booking in clients at times and days convenient to you, generally living the life!

Whilst some of this may be true to a degree, the reality, especially in the first few years of business, is that you work as hard as you can to build up your clientele, working at times and days convenient to your clients, squeezing in clients when you would normally have a break or at the end of the day and doing this at least six days a week.

When I first decided I wanted to be a therapist full-time, I was trying to expand my client list and working at three separate clinics. I would travel from one end of London to another to see maybe only one or two clients – this wasn't particularly an effective use of my time but the clinic receptionists knew they could rely on me to turn up and therefore I was a reliable therapist to them and one they could call upon when they had someone in front of them or on the phone who needed a treatment.

An example of this is on one particular day, after having treated a couple of clients in the afternoon, I was on the bus heading home when I received a call from the receptionist of that same clinic. Someone had called the clinic, desperate for a treatment (as most clients usually are!), and was I still in the area? I wanted to go home but didn't want to lose the opportunity to treat a new client, so I got off the bus and got another one back to the clinic! This benefited us all in several ways – I got to meet and treat a new client, the client was grateful to the clinic for finding someone and the receptionist was able to help out the potential customer. Subsequently, the receptionist was more likely to call me than another therapist as I was more reachable and likely to say yes.

Never underestimate the influence of the "gate-keeper" of the clinic, i.e. the receptionist, as they filter the calls and enquiries and can channel custom your way. Ideally, you should offer them a free treatment so they have first-hand experience of your massage and can recommend you from personal experience rather than hearsay.

Whilst it is important to work very hard in the first two or three years of business, working every hour possible can be exhausting and unsustainable. I would discourage therapists from working flat out all the time. Self-employed workers generally have a tendency to accept all work that comes their way as there is a wholly reasonable fear that "you never know if any work is round the corner, so take what you can when you can". Whilst this is a powerful motivator when building your business, it can leave you feeling drained and exhausted if it continues for long periods.

As you get busier, ensure that you have adequate breaks throughout the day and try not to treat too many people in one day as this can impact both your body (physical tiredness) and energy (mental tiredness). Each therapist has their own limit depending on their physical stamina and energy required to deliver their particular treatment, so find your comfortable limit and try not to exceed it too often.

During my massage training we asked one of my college tutors what she thought might be the ideal amount of clients to treat in a day and she recommended around five hours of massage, based on endeavouring to get longevity out of your body. The amount of money needed to be earned will also dictate this according to needs and commitments but try and find your "number" and if you are able, book your diary accordingly. I currently have a maximum limit of around seven hours per day but this can and does fluctuate throughout the week.

The bigger picture of managing your own time is planning days off, holidays and building in some sort of contingency in case of illness (your own or a loved one) and emergency absences.

Days off/holidays

These need to be planned well in advance, before any clients have been booked in, so there is no need to cancel bookings. Try not to take too many too close together as clients have a limited tolerance as to how available you are and may look elsewhere if you are constantly absent.

My busiest time of the year is May to July and the weeks before Easter and Christmas so I try not to take any time off around those times. Sometimes it is unavoidable but infrequency is the key here so just don't make a habit of it.

Illness/emergency absence

This may be your own illness or that of someone close to you or any unforeseen absence such as school emergencies, accidents/incidents of someone close, etc.

Obviously this cannot be planned for but ringing any booked clients with as much notice as possible and speaking to them in person will minimise any discontent with clientele. Honesty is the best policy with these issues and people are usually empathic when you are up-front with them about the problem – don't go into too much detail but enough so clients understand your situation and any difficulties you may have. If you are able, re-book them there and then but if that's not possible due to the circumstances, make a note of who you have had to cancel and keep them posted of your availability.

Depending on your work situation and professional network, you may be able to recommend other therapists to your clients whilst you are away, or even employ someone on a temporary basis to look after your client list in your absence.

Around the weeks before Christmas, a very close family member was taken into hospital with a very serious condition. I worked out the visiting hours and managed to work a few hours each day and still visit the hospital on a daily basis. Tragically my family member passed but I chose to only tell a select number of clients with whom I had a good relationship and they were extremely supportive and understanding over the next few very difficult weeks. I took some time off before and after the funeral but still needed to work but being realistic about the hours and emotional toll working with such stress would take. I chose not to treat any new clients and to only book in clients that knew me well. I found that work kept me on an even keel during a very tumultuous time and by working just enough to cover expenses, I also avoided having to deal with the stress of no money coming in.

I have also had to juggle work around significant health issues and operations whilst working. Again, I tried to be realistic as to how much I could do and avoided booking clients very close together to give me time to rest in between treatments.

Although nursing staff recommended me discontinuing work for that period of time I found, yet again, that work helped keep me sane - I enjoy a structured day and the thought of sitting around all day "taking it easy" filled me with horror! I did cut back on work hours and sometimes could only treat maybe a couple of clients a day but that allowed me to focus on them instead of my health issues for a change, as well as keeping the waiting list of clients down to a minimum and earning enough to cover costs - a build-up of waiting clients is as stressful to me as no clients at all.

Obviously sick days are determined by the illness and the therapist's tolerance but the message is don't push yourself too hard and only you can decide what that limit is - hopefully you're in it for the long term and you need to pace yourself in our industry otherwise burn-out is inevitable.

If possible, I strongly recommend that you put aside a regular amount of money to allow for unforeseen time off. You should try to have at least a month's worth of takings saved as a safety net for loss of earnings due to any of the above. It is sometimes worth contacting the Department of Works and Pensions if it looks like you are going to be unable to work for an extended period of time but be warned, the allowance is minimal and may lead to austere financial adjustments. Remember, even though you may not be able to work, the bills will keep on coming!

On a much more positive note, being self-employed does have huge benefits, and if you plan properly and treat your clients and their time with the respect and consideration they deserve, you can have a very flexible and rewarding working life!

ACKNOWLEDGEMENTS

I would like to thank all the wonderful clients that I have treated throughout the years and to thank them for all the amazing stories we have shared together and that make my work so fulfilling and fascinating.

I have been very fortunate to work with outstanding professionals, both at college and in my work life, and thank them for being so generous with their knowledge, experience and wisdom.

Finally, thanks to my husband, Andrew, for initiating this project in the first place and for all his support, encouragement and belief. A big thank you to Aliki (aka Sibling) for her patience and help in proof-reading and editing.

I would like to dedicate this book to my parents, Antigoni and Theofilaktos, for teaching me that hard work and good manners go a long way to success!

If you have any further comments or questions, please feel free to contact me:

phaedradyke@gmail.com

LINKS AND RESOURCES

CPDs (Continual Professional Development courses)

www.lssm.com

www.nlssm.com

www.jingmassage.com

www.bodyworkcpd.co.uk

www.bluechipmassage.co.uk

www.physiouk.co.uk

Equipment suppliers

MarshCouch – www.marshcouch.com – portable and fixed couches

Galleon Supplies - www.galleonsupplies.co.uk – all hygiene supplies including good quality couch rolls, gloves, wipes

Physique Management – www.physique.co.uk – comprehensive supplier for the therapist including equipment, massage oils, gloves, taping etc

Boiance face cradle available from www.oakworks.com or www.massagetablestore.com

First Aid courses

www.firstaidtraining.co.uk

www.redcrossfirstaidtraining.co.uk

www.sja.org.uk

Magazine subscriptions

Massage World Magazine - www.massageworld.co.uk

Massage and Bodywork Magazine – www.massageandbodywork.com

Holistic Therapy Magazine – www.holistictherapistmagazine.com

Journal of Bodywork and Movement Therapies - www.journals.elsevier.com

Massage Associations

ISRM – Institute of Sports and Remedial Massage www.isrm.com

CNHC – Complementary & Natural Healthcare Council www.cnhc.org.uk

LSSM – London School of Sports Massage www.lssm.com

NLSSM – North London School of Sports Massage www.nlssm.com

BTPA – Bowen Therapy Professional Association www.bowen-therapy.co

AOR – Association of Reflexology www.aor.org.uk

ATC – Aromatherapy Trade Council www.a-t-c.org.uk

SS -Shiatsu Society www.shiatsusociety.org

TTYMA –Traditional Thai Yoga Massage Association www.ttyma.co.uk

MTUK – Massage Therapy UK www.massagetherapy.co.uk

Miscellaneous sites

Insurance – www.balens.co.uk

Tax and National Insurance – www.hmrc.gov.uk

Employment information and benefits – www.gov.uk

(Business and Self-employed)

(Working, jobs and pensions)

Business plans – www.princes-trust.org.uk

www.bplans.co.uk